GOGO

AND THE TEDDY BEARS' PICNIC

JONATHAN GUNSON
WRITER & ILLUSTRATOR

RICHARD ROBINSON
ILLUSTRATOR

ISBN 978-0-473-58755-0

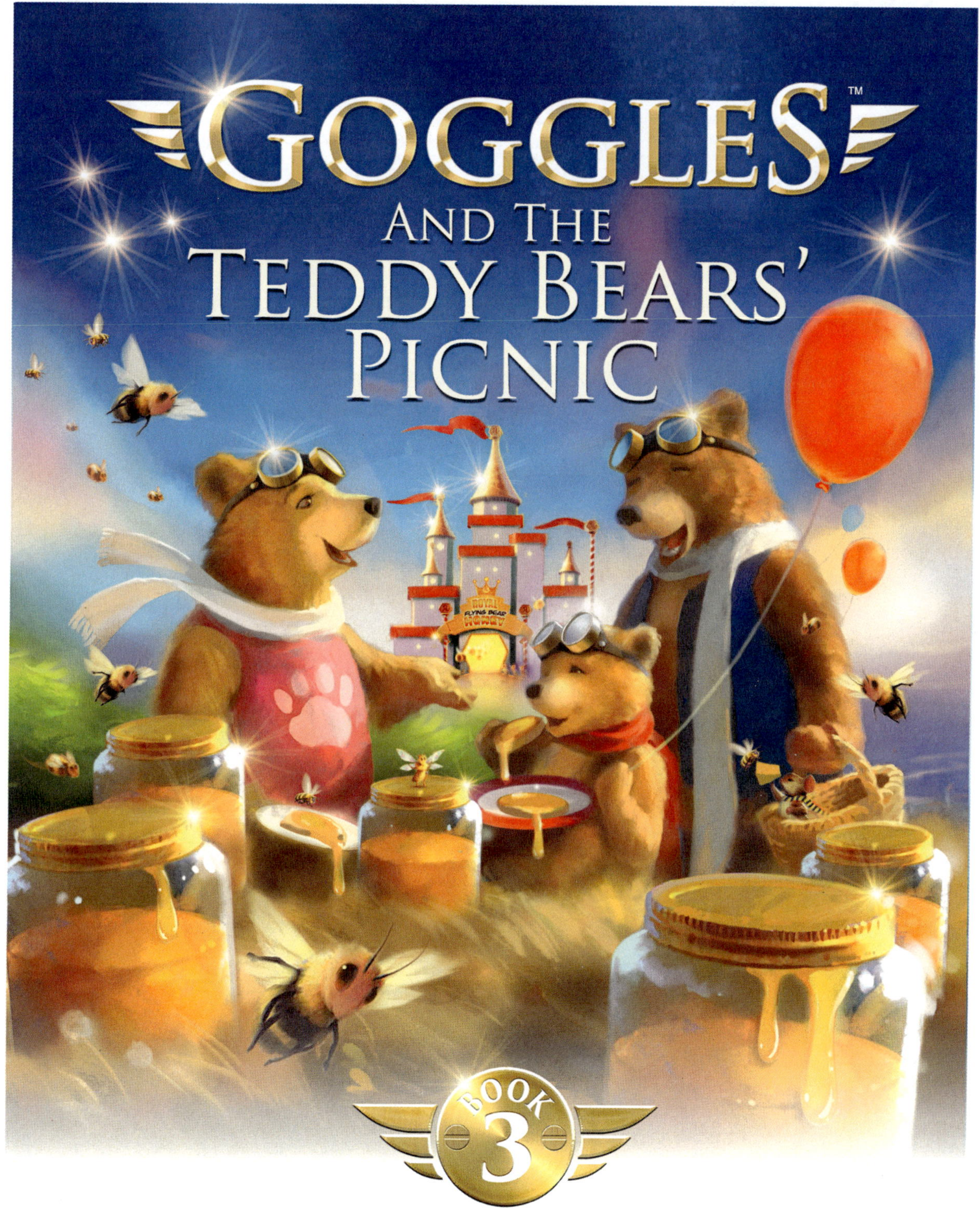

Written by Jonathan Gunson

Illustrations by Richard Robinson
& Jonathan Gunson

There was once a very small bear who loved flying so much, he wore flying goggles everywhere. So all his family called him 'Goggles'.

But even though he was a very small bear,
he had a BIG secret – a toy Bearplane that could
magically change to any size, and fly
to wherever he liked.

Goggles and his loving grandparents, Growlville and Wilma Wright, were the first bears to fly.

Every day they flew in their honey-powered 'Wright Flyer' plane to the beehives in Wildflower Meadow, where their friends the Honey Bees made honey for them.

FLYING BEAR
HONEY

But one evening, a huge storm blew up.

The beehives began to tumble down
in the wild wind and rain.

FLYING BEAR
HONEY

Work began at sunrise on building the new Honey Bee Palace.

And for years after, little bear cubs would sing the song of how it was built in just one day.

"Goggles brought his
hammer and saw,
Growly, Growly BEAR!"

"Grandpa made the
palace door,
Growly, Growly BEAR!"

"Sparky Bear did glittery lights, and Plumber Bear had colorful pipes."

"And all of them said "Growly, Growly BEAR!"

"Glazier Bear put glass
in the towers,
Growly, Growly BEAR!"
"Grandma planted
beautiful flowers,
Growly, Growly BEAR!"

"Roofing Bear made a roof in the sky, and Builder Bear built the walls up high."

"And all of them said Growly, Growly BEAR!"

It was a race against time, but just as the sun was setting, the Honey Bee Palace was finished.

The Queen and her royal family of honey bees all cheered, and flew excitedly into their new home.

BUZZZZZ!

ROYAL
FLYING BEAR
HONEY

That night at bedtime, Grandma gave Goggles a big hug. "Time for little bears to rest," she said.

"You worked so hard today, and the honey bees are STILL working! They're building the Queen Bee's Throne Room."

“Ooooh ... can I see it?” asked Goggles, excitedly.

“It's hidden inside the palace. Only honey bees are small enough to visit,” said Grandma.

Goggles woke early the next day. He pushed the secret button in his magical Bearplane.

It quickly grew to full size and the pilot's door swung open. "Welcome aboard," said the Bearplane. "Where would you like to fly?"

“I would love to see Queen Honey Bee’s Throne Room,” said Goggles. “Let's shrink to bee size so we can sneak in.”

He pushed the ‘shrink’ button and the plane shrank to bee size, disguised with honey bee colors.

Goggles hit the GO! button

With a whizz and a whirr, the propeller began to spin.
He lifted off for his secret flight to the Honey Bee palace.

He buzzed downstairs into the kitchen.
The Bearplane was so small, Grandma and Grandpa didn't even see it. They just smiled because they thought a Honey Bee was buzzing by.

Goggles flew out the window, and headed for Wildflower Meadow.

... ZOOOM!

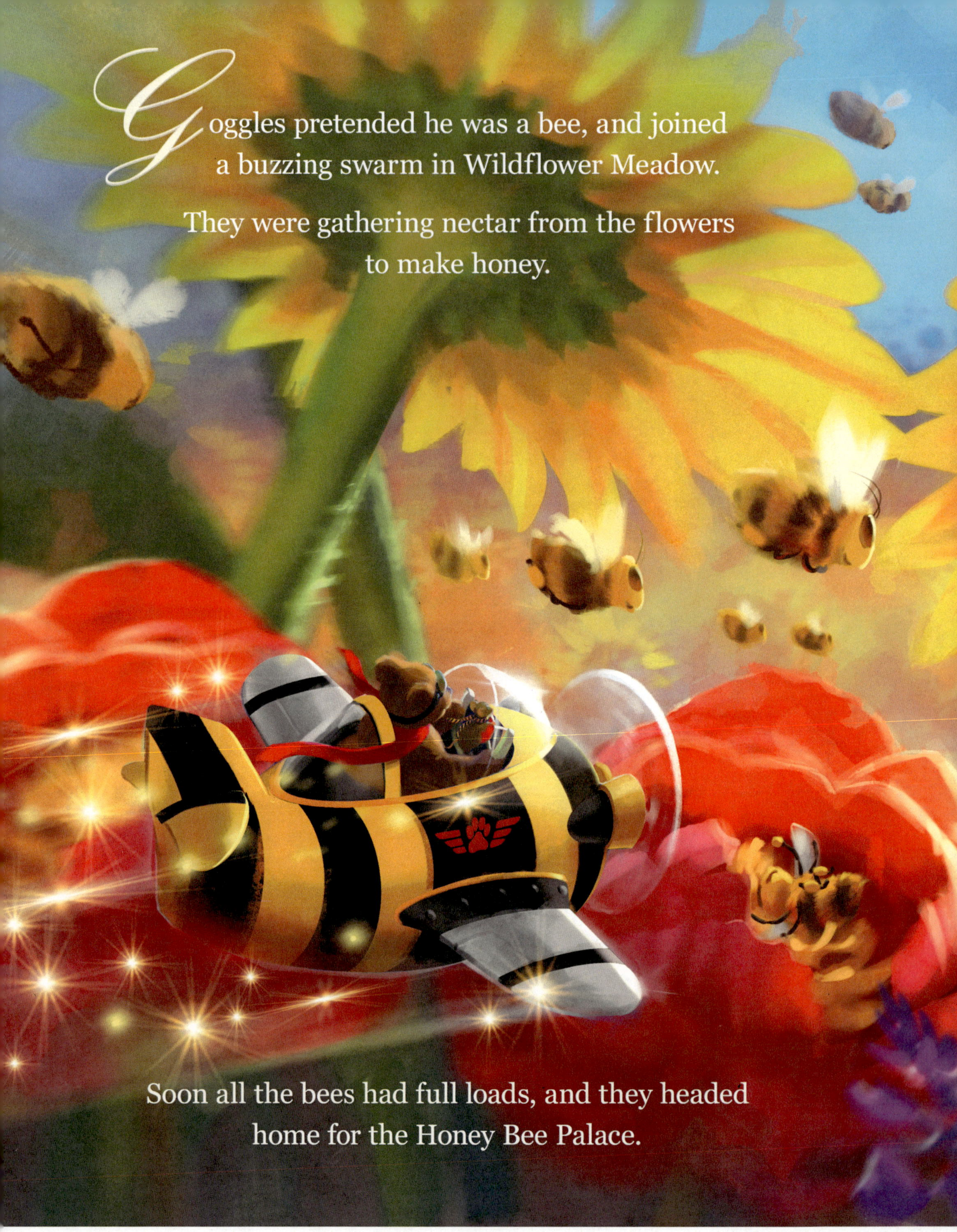

Goggles pretended he was a bee, and joined a buzzing swarm in Wildflower Meadow.

They were gathering nectar from the flowers to make honey.

Soon all the bees had full loads, and they headed home for the Honey Bee Palace.

ROYAL
FLYING BEAR
HONEY

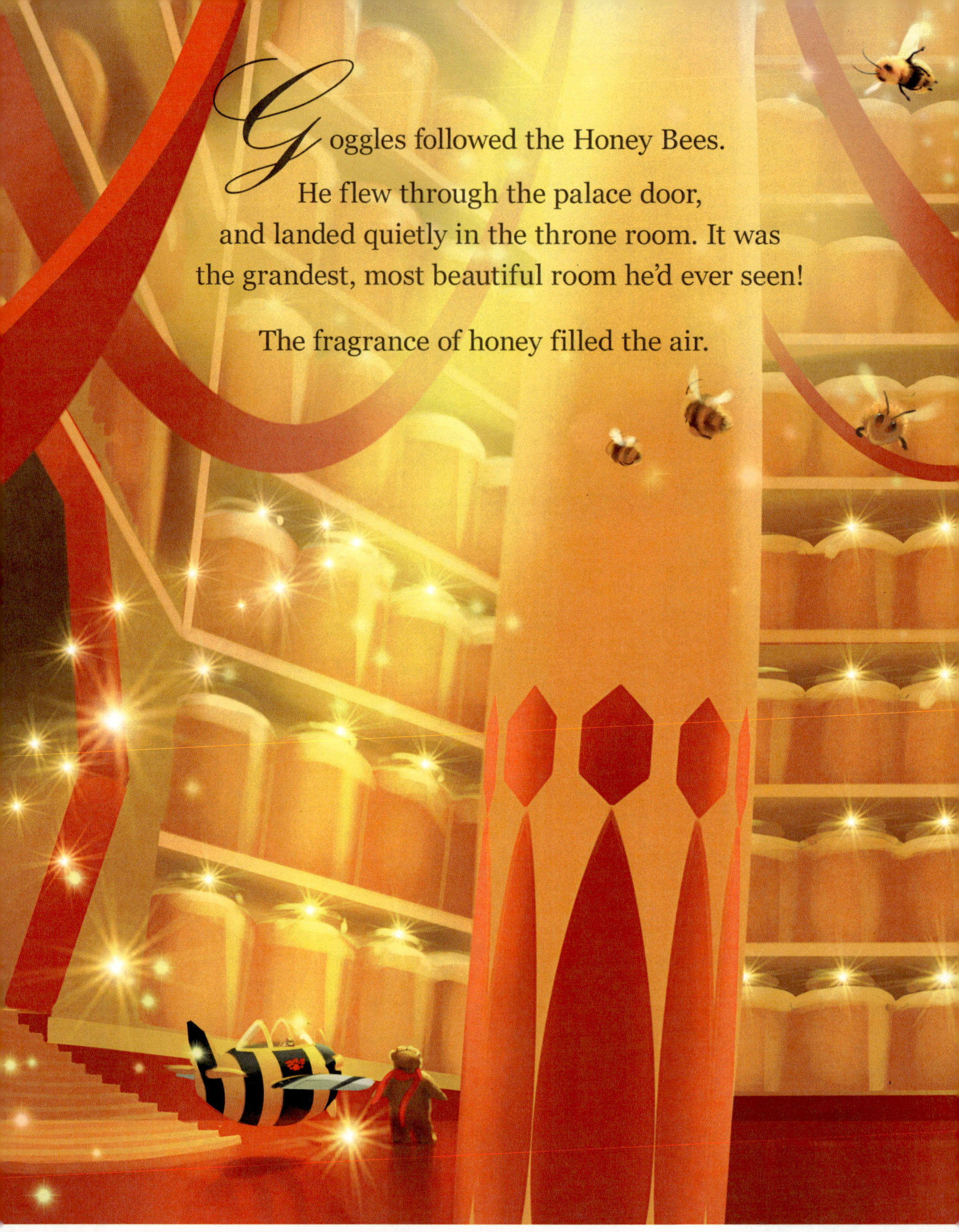

Goggles followed the Honey Bees.
He flew through the palace door,
and landed quietly in the throne room. It was
the grandest, most beautiful room he'd ever seen!

The fragrance of honey filled the air.

Suddenly, Goggles was captured by the palace guards. "You're not a Honey Bee! You're a honey spy!" they shouted.

But Queen Honey Bee appeared.
"Release him!" she commanded. "It's Goggles.
He helped build our beautiful palace."

"Why are you so incredibly small?" she asked him.

"I shrank to bee size so I could see your
throne room," said Goggles.

Queen Honey Bee smiled. “If I keep your Bearplane a secret, will you promise to keep my throne room a secret too ?

“I PROMISE!” said Goggles.

“Now tell me,” she asked, “how can I thank all the lovely bears who built our new home?”

And right then, Goggles had one of his greatest ideas ever. He whispered it in the Queen's ear. Can you guess what it was?

At breakfast the next day, a large golden invitation with a royal seal arrived at the Wright Bears' family home.

"It's from Queen Honey Bee," said Grandma excitedly.

The Wright Bears
are invited to a
Secret Party
at noon today

~Queen Honey Bee~
Royal Honey Bee Palace
Wild Flower Meadow

"OOOOOH!" said Grandpa. "I wonder what the secret party is ?"

But Goggles knew. After all, it was his best idea ever.

At noon, the bears landed their plane in Wildflower Meadow.

Queen Honey Bee welcomed them with a surprise TEDDY BEARS' PICNIC!

There was honey for all to say thank you for the Honey Bee Palace.

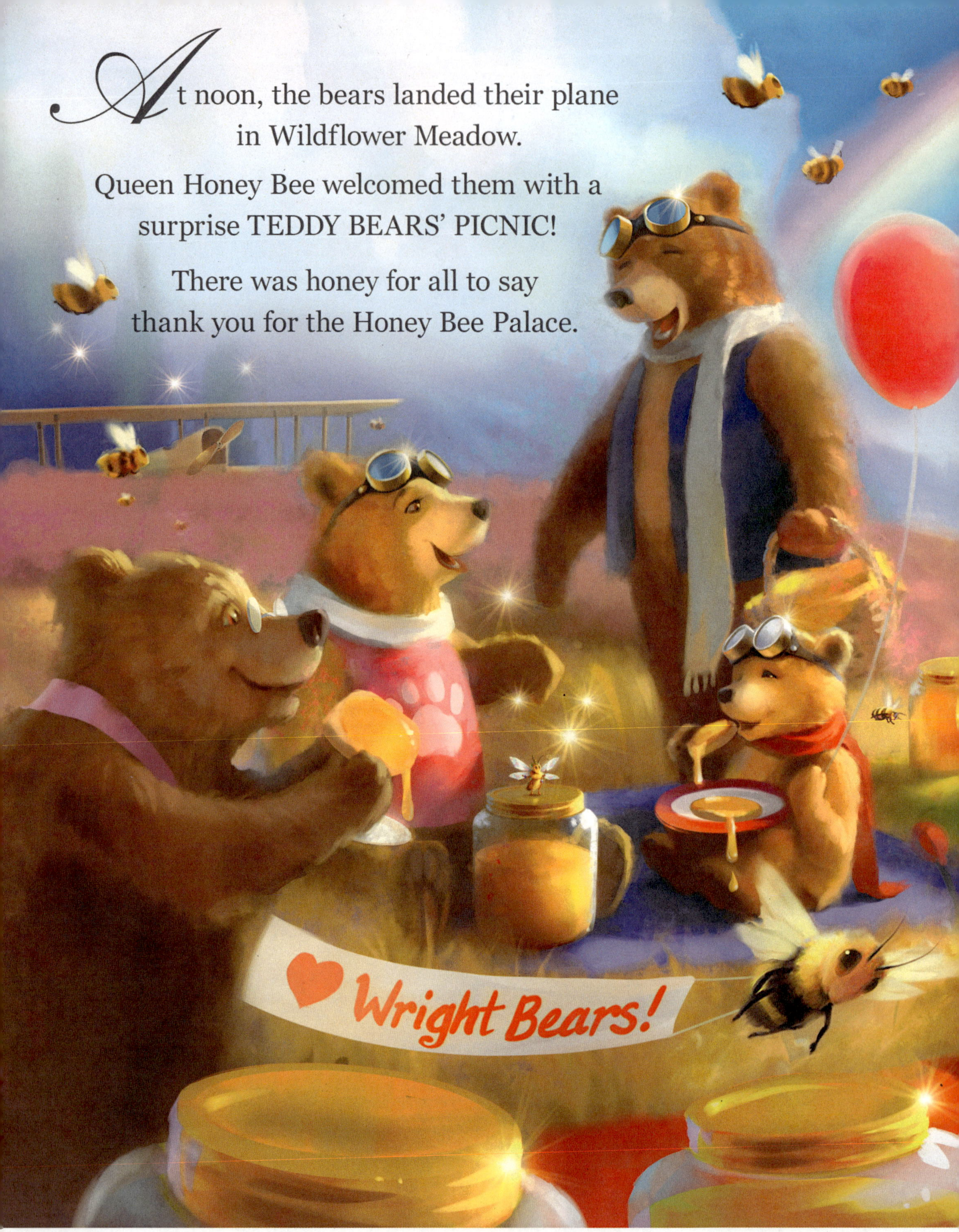

Welcome!
THE GRAND
TEDDY BEARS' PICNIC
"Say cheese!"

That night, Grandma Wilma whispered wistfully, "I wonder what Queen Honey Bee's throne room is like? It must be so beautiful."

But Goggles just smiled; it was his secret, and it had been a lovely day.

"I won't
squeak!"

GOGGLES™
Guide To
The Beehive

Honey Bees collect nectar from flowers, and take it back to the beehive where it is made into honey.

Beehives in a meadow of *Phacelia* flowers with nectar that Honey Bees collect

A beekeeper harvests a beehive frame full of honey

A Beehive is a special house where Honey Bees make honey and raise baby bees.

Bees make honey from a sweet syrup called nectar they find in flowers. Honey Bees collect nectar all summer and take it back to their Beehive home, where worker bees turn it into honey to live on during the winter.

On the top floor, bees make hexagonal shaped wax cells on frames and fill them with honey. (A hexagon has six sides.)

Beekeepers harvest the frames of honey, but leave enough for the bees to live on during the winter.

The "Queen excluder" has little holes that allow the small Honey Bees into the top floor. The big Queen Bee can't get through to lay eggs, so the top floor contains only pure honey, making it easier for beekeepers to collect.

The middle floor is a nursery for the baby bees, where the Queen lays eggs in the same type of wax cells as the top floor.

At the bottom of the beehive is the front door, a long narrow slot with a small entrance so the Honey Bees can safely come and go.

Bees make so much honey, there's plenty for humans (and bears) as well.

GOGGLES
THE TEDDY BEARS' PICNIC
COLORING BOOK
GOGGLES
FIRST BEAR TO FLY
GOGGLES
FIRST BEAR TO FLY

FREE COLORING PAGES!

Get this whole book
"Goggles and the Teddy Bears' Picnic" as coloring pages
and enjoy it all over again!

FREE AT THIS WEBSITE:

www.colorbook.fun